THIRTY-TWO MOONS
THE NATURAL SATELLITES
OF OUR SOLAR SYSTEM

THIRTY-TWO MOONS

THE NATURAL SATELLITES OF OUR SOLAR SYSTEM

BY DAVID C. KNIGHT

illustrated with photographs,
drawings by Pamela Carroll,
and diagrams by Ellen Cullen

WILLIAM MORROW AND COMPANY
New York 1974

*The 120-inch telescope at Lick Observatory,
Mount Hamilton, California.*

Printed in the United States of America.
1   2   3   4   5   78   77   76   75   74

Library of Congress Cataloging Publication Data

Knight, David C
    Thirty-two moons.

    SUMMARY: Discusses the possible origins, the composition, and the characteristics of each of the thirty-two known natural satellites in the solar system.
    1. Satellites—Juvenile literature. [1. Satellites. 2. Solar system] I. Carroll, Pamela, illus. II. Cullen, Ellen, illus. III. Title.
QB401.K58   523.9′8   73-13046
ISBN 0-688-20110-5
ISBN 0-688-30110-X (lib. bdg.)

Picture credits:
Lick Observatory, University of California, frontispiece, page 85; NASA, pages 17, 18, 24, 26, 32, 33, 38, 39; Yerkes Observatory, University of Chicago, pages 44, 49, 61 (photographed by E. C. Slipher), 78 (photo-graphed by G. P. Kuiper)

By the same author:

THE TINY PLANETS,
Asteroids of Our Solar System

CONTENTS

OUR SOLAR SYSTEM'S THIRTY-TWO MOONS

Now that earthmen have landed on the natural satellite of their own planet, they may one day visit the natural satellites of other planets in the solar system.

In the case of four—Jupiter, Saturn, Uranus, and Neptune—earthmen will probably get no closer than their satellites. Landing on these giant planets, with their intensely cold temperatures and forbidding, gaseous atmospheres, would be difficult indeed. Even if earthmen accomplished such landings, they would find that attempting to live and work there for any length of time would be impracticable.

Earthmen, however, will be able to observe and study these planets in another way. Jupiter has twelve satellites; Saturn, ten; Uranus, five; and Neptune, two. It will be from one or more of these natural satellites, perpetually orbiting their primaries, or parent bodies, that men will be able to observe these four largest worlds of the sun's family.

Astronomers define a natural satellite as a celestial body that revolves around one of the planets of the solar system. The moon is the earth's natural satellite. By analogy, the natural satellites of other planets are often called "moons"

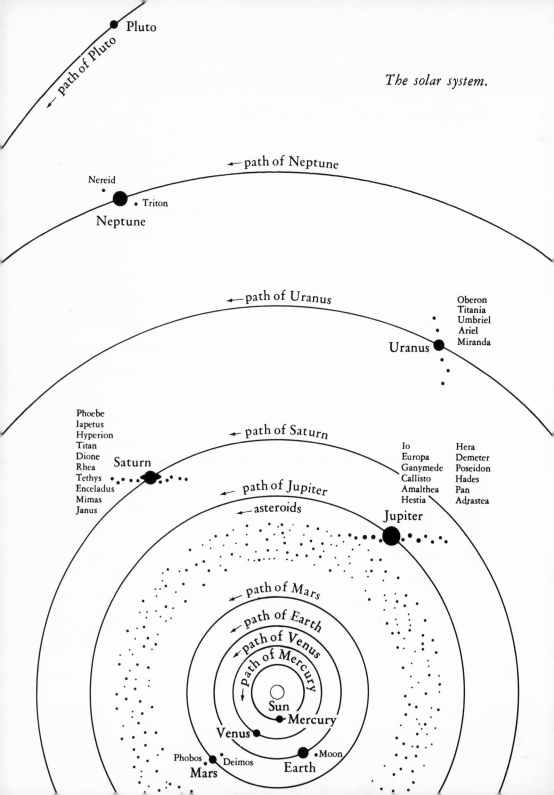

The solar system.

in popular scientific literature, although astronomers prefer the term *natural satellite*.

Besides the earth and the four giant planets, one other planet possesses a satellite system. It is Mars, which has two small moons. The remaining planets—Mercury, Venus, and Pluto—have no known natural satellites.

In all, there are thirty-two known moons orbiting the planets of the solar system. Some are very small, no more than 10 miles or so in diameter. But six are as large or larger than our own moon, which has a diameter of 2160 miles. Like the earth's moon, most of the other thirty-one are probably barren, bleak worlds, although none are believed to have atmospheres. They are also bitterly cold for at such vast distances from the sun they receive very little light and heat.

Technically there are many more than thirty-two natural satellites in the solar system. The rings of Saturn consist of countless millions of tiny particles—most thought to be ice-coated bits of rock. Each is really a miniscule satellite of this giant planet. Nor is it certain that Pluto, discovered as late as 1930, is the last planet in the solar system. If it is not, still more distant planets may be discovered that possess moons.

How did the thirty-two moons originate? Why do some planets have several? Why do some have none? At present,

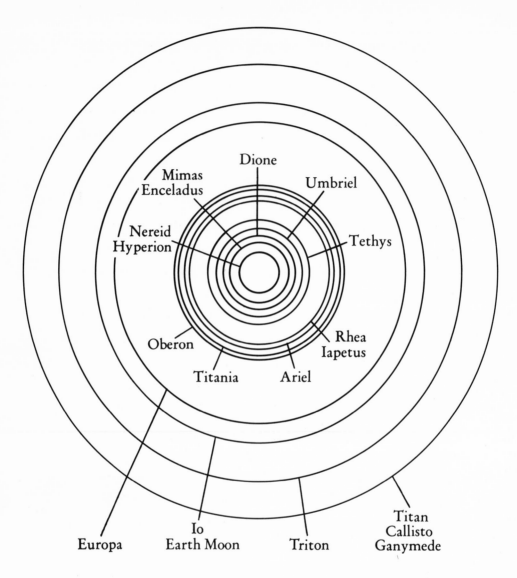

Mimas
Enceladus
Dione
Umbriel
Nereid
Hyperion
Tethys
Oberon
Rhea
Iapetus
Titania
Ariel

Europa
Io
Earth Moon
Triton
Titan
Callisto
Ganymede

Relative sizes of thirty-two moons.

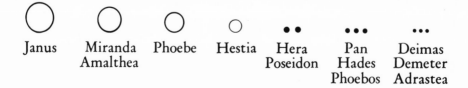

Janus
Miranda
Amalthea
Phoebe
Hestia
Hera
Poseidon
Pan
Hades
Phoebos
Deimas
Demeter
Adrastea

scientists cannot answer these questions because they are not in agreement about how the solar system itself originated.

In the last 200 years of scientific thought, there have been approximately half a dozen serious theories proposed to explain the origin of the solar system. Today scientists tend to favor two of these, or variations of them, and they may offer a clue as to how the thirty-two moons themselves might have originated.

One modern hypothesis of the origin of the solar system was proposed by the American astronomer Gerard P. Kuiper. He assumed there was originally a disk-shaped nebula (a gaseous cloud) of tremendous extent, with the protosun (the sun-to-be) at its center. The overall composition of the nebula was uniform, and its temperature was low because the protosun had not yet begun to radiate by thermonuclear reaction. This cold nebula began to break up and concentrate into separate masses—the protoplanets, or planets-to-be. Eventually the material at the center (the protosun) became concentrated under the force of gravitation. As it shrank, it became hotter and hotter. Then radiation from the protosun drove most of the lighter elements (particularly hydrogen and helium) out of the protoplanets and the nebula itself. In each protoplanet, most of the heavier elements such as iron and nickel concentrated toward the center. As the protoplanets decreased in size, they

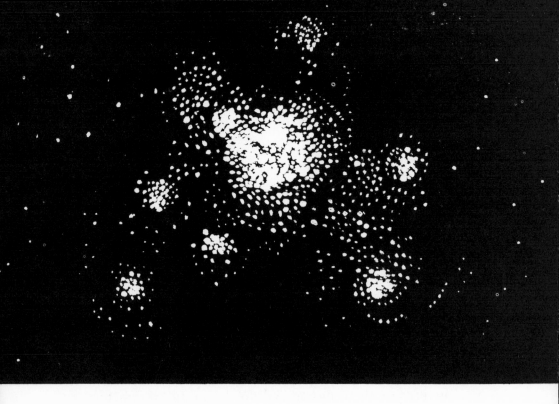

*Kuiper's disk-shaped nebular hypothesis
of the origin of the solar system.*

began to rotate faster, attaining much the same rotational
speed they have today. With this increase in their spinning,
material may have been thrown off them, forming satellites.

The other theory now favored by many scientists is the
dust-and-gas-cloud hypothesis. According to the American
astronomer Fred L. Whipple, who proposed it, the solar
system-to-be was at first a vast cloud of cosmic dust and gas.

*Whipple's dust-and-gas-cloud hypothesis
of the origin of the solar system.*

Local irregularities, inevitable in such a dispersed cloud, gradually produced rotation and led to the cloud's collapsing inward on itself under its own gravitation. As it did so, the dust and gas became more concentrated. The more solid particles in the cloud collided, stuck together, balled up, and eventually became the planets, while the larger concentration of collapsing gases at the center formed the sun. The

13

present-day planetary satellites may have been smaller fragments that did not merge with the major planets but later became captured in orbits about their parent bodies.

Exactly how the solar system *was* formed is a question that is far from settled. And indeed, just how the natural satellites themselves came into being may forever remain an astronomical mystery. Nevertheless, the thirty-two moons exist, and they are potentially important members of the sun's family.

THE EARTH
AND ITS
MOON

Earth, our home planet, is unique in the solar system for three reasons. It is the only planet known to possess intelligent life. It is the only planet to have large amounts of liquid water on its surface covering nearly three fourths of its crust. And it is the only planet that possesses a single natural satellite, the moon.

As the moon's primary, the earth is the third planet from the sun. Its mean, or average, distance from the sun is about 92,870,000 miles. Earth's period of revolution around the sun, or its year, is 365 days, and its rotational period, or day, about its axis is 23 hours and 56 minutes. The earth has an atmosphere of about 700 miles in depth, which consists of nitrogen, oxygen, water vapor, and other gases. Its diameter is nearly 8000 miles.

Compared with its sister planets, Venus and Mars, the earth is massive. Astronomers use the term *mass* to describe this characteristic of a heavenly body. Mass means the total amount of matter that a planet contains; it is measured in terms of units such as tons. The mass of the earth is 6 sextillion tons (1 sextillion is the number 1 followed by 21 zeroes). Venus, which is about the same size as the earth, is only .81 of the earth's mass. Mars, though half the size of the earth, is still only .11 the mass of earth.

This massiveness of the earth explains in large part why it is able to "hold on" to—by gravitational attraction—such a comparatively big satellite as the moon, which has a diameter of 2160 miles. By comparison, Mars, with its small mass, could not hold a body with a size comparable to that of our moon.

Thus, the large mass of the moon in relation to the earth makes the earth-moon system like no others in the solar system. Actually, our moon is only the sixth largest of the thirty-two. Three of Jupiter's and one each of Saturn's and Neptune's are larger. But compared to its primary, the earth, the moon is the largest of all.

So large is the moon in relation to the earth that some scientists call the earth-moon system a double planet. The moon differs from the true planets only by the fact that it is in orbit around the earth; were it following an independent path about the sun, it would be a full-fledged planet. A viewer of the earth-moon system from Venus would see it very much as a double planet.

Oddly, the length of the moon's day and its year with respect to its primary are the same. This is because its period of rotation on its axis (the day) and its period of revolution

An outstanding view of a full moon taken by Apollo 11.

An Apollo 16 view of a near-full moon. Most of the lunar area shown here is on the dark side of the moon.

around the earth (the year) are equal—27 earth days, 7 hours, and 43 minutes. Hence, observers on earth always see the same side of the moon. Before an unmanned Soviet lunar probe photographed the "dark side" of the moon in the 1960's, no human being had ever seen it.

The moon is the closest celestial body to the earth, orbiting it at a mean distance of about 239,000 miles. But once each month during its journey around the earth it comes a few thousand miles closer to the earth; and once each month it wanders out a few thousand miles beyond the mean distance. This is because the moon—like all bodies in the solar system—travels in an elliptical orbit, or path, around its primary. No known celestial body travels in a perfect circle around its primary but in an ellipse, an elongated or slightly "squashed" circle.

The moon is visible, as are the earth and other planets, because it reflects the light radiating from the sun. However, the moon is a relatively poor reflector; it reflects only about 7 percent of the sunlight that falls upon it.

The different shapes in which we see the moon in the sky are called its "phases." They are due to the varying amounts of the sunlit lunar surface that we see as the moon revolves about the earth once each month. At full moon, the earth is between the sun and the moon, but the inclination of the moon's orbit to that of the earth usually positions the moon

19

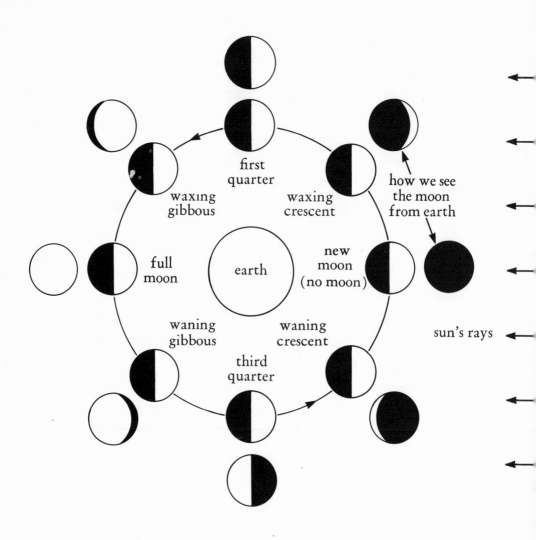

first
quarter

waxing
gibbous

waxing
crescent

how we see
the moon
from earth

full
moon

earth

new
moon
(no moon)

waning
gibbous

waning
crescent

sun's rays

third
quarter

The phases of the moon.

outside of the earth's shadow, and the whole lunar disk facing the earth is illuminated. At new moon, the moon is between the sun and the earth, and the sun's rays illuminate only the hemisphere facing the sun, leaving the side facing the earth in complete darkness and making it invisible from earth. After new moon, the waxing, or growing, thin crescent turns into first quarter. Following the full moon, the waning, or lessening, gibbous ("humpbacked") phase turns into last quarter, then into new moon again.

To observers on earth, the motion of the moon occasionally produces two kinds of eclipses. Eclipses of the sun are caused when the moon passes between the earth and the sun and is at or near the point where its orbit crosses the earth's. Then it casts a shadow that extends to the earth. Eclipses of the moon itself are seen when the earth is between the sun and

Eclipse of the sun.

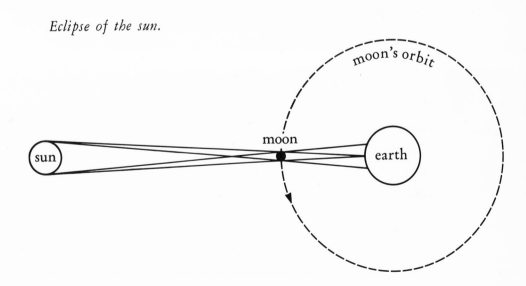

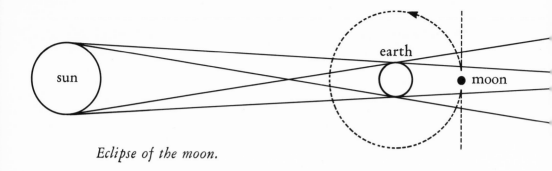

Eclipse of the moon.

the moon, and the moon is at or near the crossing point of the orbits.

The mass of the moon is only ⅟₈₁ that of the earth. Its surface gravity is but ⅙ of the earth's, which means that a 150-pound man weighs only 25 pounds on the moon. Because of this reduced gravity the astronauts on the lunar surface seem to bound and even float along.

Since the moon has no atmosphere, sunlight on the moon is very bright and shadows are absolutely black. Why? Because no earthlike blanket of air molecules can filter the sun's rays and insulate the moon as those rays mercilessly beat down on the lunar surface. The lack of atmosphere on the moon also makes its surface temperatures very severe. Near the lunar equator, at noontime, rocks would be above the boiling point of water (270 degrees Fahrenheit); at midnight, temperatures fall as low as minus 215 degrees Fahrenheit.

As seen through binoculars, the rough lunar surface resembles a ravaged wasteland. It is divided into bright highland areas comprising about two thirds of the total surface and dark lowland plains called *"maria"* (Latin for "seas") because they were originally thought to be lunar oceans. (The name is actually a misnomer since there is no water on the surface of the moon.)

Craters are the most conspicuous and plentiful of all the moon's surface features. Thousands of them dot the lunar surface. Some are believed to have resulted from volcanic activity within the moon, and some are doubtless the result of meteoroids impacting on the moon's crust. Craters may also have formed from collapsing material triggered by moonquakes.

Because the craters are far more numerous in the highland areas than in the low-lying *maria,* scientists think that the dark *maria* developed relatively late in the crater-forming history of the moon. Otherwise, they would contain far more craters than they do. The *maria* appear to be like giant lava plains that resemble lava beds on earth.

Rills, or deep canyons, are another feature of the lunar surface. Some are more than 100 miles long. It is believed that the moon originally had water trapped in its interior, as did the earth. Some scientists believe that after this water was forced out of the interior in the form of vapor, it was quickly lost into space before it could accumulate on the surface. Others think that water remained long enough to flow and carve out the rills. At present, the origin of the rills remains a mystery.

In 1968, small changes of motion in the unmanned Lunar Orbiter 5 spacecraft were picked up by scientists on earth. These movements revealed the presence of large concentrations of massive material in the moon's crust. The scientists named them *mascons* (after *mas*s *con*centration*s*). Five conspicuous ones, ranging from 25 to 100 miles in extent and perhaps 25 miles below the surface, were detected under all five large circular *maria* on the side of the moon facing

Mascons (ringed in white and in black circles) were discovered through analysis of tracking data from the Lunar Orbiter missions.

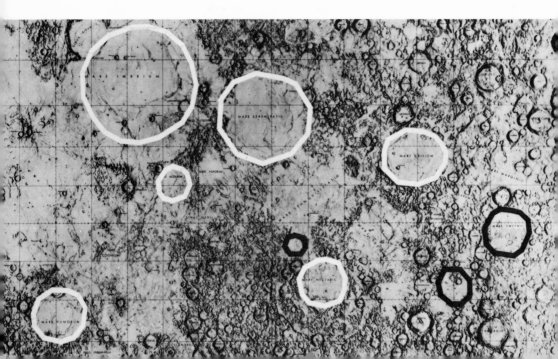

earth. Later, more mascons were found under other *maria* by spacecraft orbiting the moon.

Scientists were able to detect these mascons because the spacecraft speeded up as they passed over them. From this observation they concluded that there were larger concentrations of material in these places and that they were exerting stronger gravitational pull on the spacecraft. Yet why, scientists asked themselves, should these large concentrations of matter exist in some places and not in others? Many think that they resulted from the impact of giant meteoroids, which embedded themselves in the lunar surface.

One of the prime missions of the manned landings on the moon by Apollo astronauts was to bring back lunar samples. These valuable collections are being studied intently by geologists and other scientists in the hope that they will turn up new knowledge about the moon's early history. Some of the specimens already studied are at least a half-billion years older than any ever found on the earth.

Specifically, what have been some of the scientific findings from the Apollo landings? Specimens collected from the lunar *maria* show that some areas are unusually rich in titanium. In addition to titanium, all of the lunar rocks were found to have high concentrations of such rare elements as scandium, zirconium, hafnium, and yttrium, though being deficient in such common earth elements as chlorine, sodium,

A sample of lunar rock collected by Apollo 12's explorers.

and potassium. One lunar area in the Copernicus crater region was found to be especially rich in radioactive uranium and thorium. Fragments of an unusually uranium-rich rock known as Kreep from the Apollo 14 and 15 sites may have been formed very early in lunar history, between 4.3 and 4.4 billion years ago. Other specimens indicate that the flooding by lava of such lunar seas as the Ocean of Storms and the Sea of Fertility occurred a billion and more years after the Kreep.

The discovery of lunar rocks as old as 4.5 million years already has cast severe doubts on one long-held theory of the moon's formation. This theory suggests that at one time in the distant past the moon and the earth were a single body rotating at very high speed. So rapid was the rotation that huge quantities of material were torn away from the earth's crust and formed the moon. The great cavity of the Pacific Ocean basin, so states the theory, was the original home of this material. But the oldest known surface rocks on earth are thought to be only a little more than 3.7 billion years old. If rocks on the moon are known to be as old as 4.5 billion years, how could they have come from the earth? All bodies of the solar system itself are thought to have formed about 4.65 billion years ago.

What does the study of these lunar samples suggest? Why the difference in age between lunar and earth rocks? Why are such elements as thorium and uranium scarce on the earth and more or less abundant on the moon? The evidence points, some scientists think, to two new variations of the gas-cloud theory of the origin of the moon.

Both these new hypotheses are derived from evidence that the moon is made largely of refractory minerals—those that melt only at very high temperatures such as thorium, titanium, and uranium. At the time the planets were forming, such substances would have been the first to condense out of the mixture of gaseous compounds thought to have been circling the sun. Substances with lower melting points would have condensed only later as the gases slowly cooled in space.

One of the new theories holds that the moon was formed in an orbital path as close to the sun as that of Mercury, the innermost planet. The theory further suggests that Mercury itself, being so close to the sun, is also formed of refractory materials. An early gravitational battle then ensued between Mercury and the moon. The more powerful gravity of Mercury, a full-fledged planet, eventually threw the moon into a new orbit that carried it out toward earth. This theory not only accounts for the older rocks of the moon, it explains the greater abundance of refractory minerals in the lunar crust.

The second of the new theories suggests that the moon formed at roughly the same distance from the sun as the earth. But it did so in an orbital path tilted sharply to the plane of the ecliptic, which is the plane of the earth's orbit around the sun. The ecliptic is also the general plane in which the other planets (except Pluto, the outermost) circle the sun—a broad disk-shaped region in which the planets originally formed. Most of the hot gas from which the planets ultimately developed is assumed to have lain in this vast disk. Above and below it, the lower gas temperature and pressure would have allowed refractory minerals to condense and cool first. Thus the newly evolving moon, which consisted of such material and whose sharply tilted orbit allowed it to escape the ecliptic region for long periods, formed before the earth did.

Whether either of these theories is correct, or whether older ones or variations of them are valid, still remains to be seen. Still unanswered is the question of just how the earth's gravity was able to attract and hold a satellite the size of the moon into a relatively circular orbit.

Many other questions about our moon also remain unanswered. For example, there is doubt about whether the moon's core is still in a molten or solid state. Seismometers —instruments designed to detect shock waves on the moon— have been set up on the lunar surface and radio information back to earth every time a moonquake or meteoroid impact occurs. Recent readings from these instruments have indicated that the lunar core is at least partially molten. But some scientists do not agree with these seismic findings and theorize that the moon's core, while hot, is not liquid.

So, despite the information gained from the Apollo landings, man's knowledge about the moon still remains meager and fragmentary. Only through future missions and intense study of the data gathered on the lunar surface will the earth's companion in space be forced to give up her secrets.

MARS
AND ITS
TWO MOONS

Mars, the fourth planet from the sun, is often called the Red
Planet because it appears that color to an observer on earth.
Its mean distance from the sun is approximately 141 million
miles.

Mars rotates eastward on its axis once every 24 hours and
37 minutes, which gives it a day that is very nearly the same
as an earth day. The planet takes 687 of our days to complete
one revolution around the sun. Thus, a year on Mars lasts
almost twice as long as a year on earth. As it speeds through
space at about 15 miles a second (a trifle slower than earth),
the Red Planet travels in a more elliptical orbit than that of
the earth.

One of the smaller planets in the sun's family, Mars has
a diameter of about 4140 miles, which is a little more than
half the earth's diameter. Like the earth, Mars is made up
of rocky material. But even if Mars were the same size as
the earth, it would not be as massive as the earth. This is
what is meant when scientists describe Mars as less dense
than the earth.

Understanding the meaning of density is important. Density is the amount of matter in a unit volume of a substance. Suppose there were two hypothetical planets, A and B. A is made of solid steel; B is made of cork. Both are exactly the same size. If one cubic mile were cut out of each planet, both cubes would occupy the same space. But obviously they would not weigh the same. The cube cut from the steel planet would weigh many times more than the cube cut from the cork planet. Or, as scientists say, the steel cube has greater density than the cork one. And since both planets are the same size, the steel planet has greater density than the one of cork.

To make density comparisons more practical, scientists use the density of water as a basis. The density of water is taken as unity, or 1. Thus, the density of the earth has been computed to be 5.5, which means that it is 5.5 times as dense as a ball of water the same size. The density of the sun is low, only 1.4 that of water. The density of the moon is 3.3.

As for Mars, its density is 3.96 that of water, which is only about 70 percent as dense as the earth. The reason for this may be that the Red Planet contains a much smaller amount of iron than the earth.

Since Mars is less massive than the earth, it has a much weaker gravitational pull. The figure for Martian surface gravity is .38, which means that bodies or objects on Mars weigh only 38 percent of what they do on earth. (Here the

Mariner Mars 1971 spacecraft.

earth is taken as unity, or 1, as a basis for comparison.)
Thus, a 100-pound earthman would weigh only 38 pounds
on the Red Planet.

During the three successful space probes of Mars by the
Mariner series of spacecraft much was learned about the
Red Planet. It was found to possess a very thin atmosphere,
containing almost no oxygen and consisting chiefly of car-
bon dioxide (CO_2). The planet's surface was well photo-

graphed by Mariners' cameras. Exciting closeup views were taken of mighty canyons, winding valleys, the polar caps, moonlike craters, huge volcanic mountains, and other surface features. From these views, scientists believe they can

Two photographs of Mars taken by Mariner 9.
Top: *A chasm with branching canyons eroding adjacent plateau lands.* Bottom: *A volcanic mountain.*

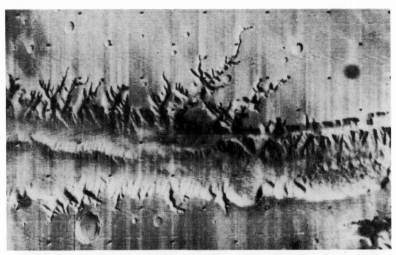

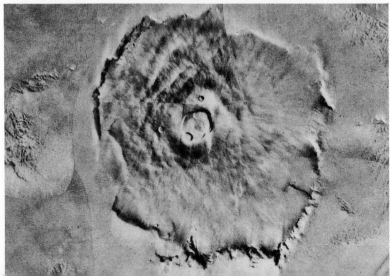

see clear-cut evidence of water-cut gulleys and other features carved by erosion, meaning that there was probably water on the Martian surface in the planet's distant past.

Mariners' cameras also radioed back to earth in November, 1971, the first pictures of the two tiny satellites of Mars: Deimos and Phobos. Curiously, these moons were objects of interest even before they were discovered in 1877.

In 1610, the German astronomer Johannes Kepler predicted by mathematical means that Mars might have two satellites. However, in his day there were no telescopes powerful enough to pick them up. Yet so sure was Kepler of his prediction that he wrote to the great Italian scientist Galileo of the probable existence of the satellites. Later the French author Voltaire, in one of his imaginative works, also mentions Mars as having two moons.

But the most incredible discovery of the two Martian satellites was made by Jonathan Swift in his famous *Gulliver's Travels,* published in the 1720's. In one of Gulliver's adventures, the two Martian satellites are described with a fair amount of accuracy. According to the story, the astronomers of Laputa (an island that was supposed to float above the earth) "discovered two lesser stars, or satellites, which revolve around Mars, whereof the innermost is distant from the center of the primary planet exactly three of its diameters, and the outermost, five; the former revolves in the

space of ten hours, and the latter in twenty-one and a half."
Actually, Swift's estimates were too great, for Phobos is
only 1.4 times the Martian diameter away from the center
of the planet, and the distance of Deimos is only 3.5 diameters. Swift's periods of revolution were off, too. Still, his
guesses were astonishingly accurate, considering the fact

*A fictional discovery of the two Martian satellites was made
by astronomers in* Gulliver's Travels, *published in the 1720's;
they were actually sighted 150 years later.*

that the moons were not actually sighted until 150 years later.

The discoverer of the two moons was Asaph Hall, an American astronomer working at the United States Naval Observatory in Washington, D.C. He was using a 26-inch telescope, then the best in existence. Hall, a master carpenter who used his trade to pay for his education in astronomy, discovered the satellites in 1877.

On the night of August 11, Hall sighted a faint object near the planet. But cloudy weather intervened, and he did not see it again until the sixteenth. Because the object was seen to be moving with the planet, there was no doubt it was a satellite and not a faint star. The next night he succeeded in locating another moon even closer to Mars. Hall named the inner satellite Phobos (Fear) and the outer one Deimos (Panic), after the companions of Mars, god of war.

The two satellites orbit the planet from west to east, which is the usual pattern for other moons in the solar system. Phobos is closer to its primary than any other known satellite in the sun's family. It is only about 5820 miles from Mars's center, which means that its distance from the Martian surface is only some 3750 miles.

Though Phobos is truly a tiny world, probably between 10 and 12 miles in diameter, a person on Mars still would

The orbits of Mars's two satellites.
Distances are approximately to scale.

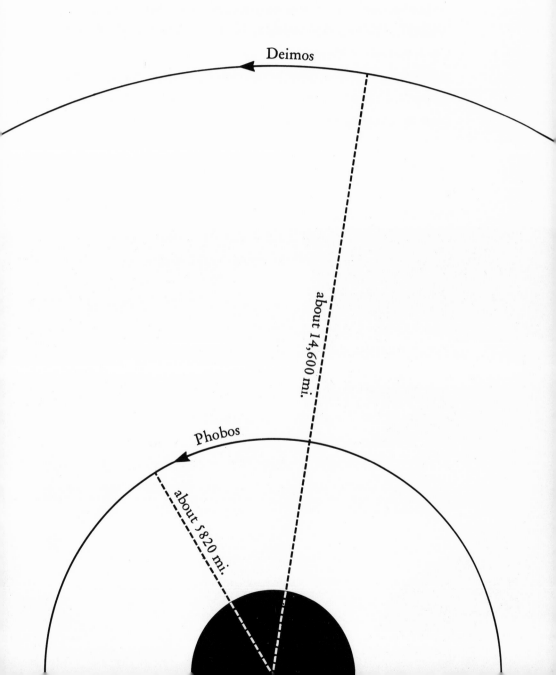

Deimos

about 14,600 mi.

Phobos

about 5820 mi.

be able to see it quite easily in the Martian sky. And it would be seen to go through phases just as our moon does. The Mariner 9 photographs of Phobos reveal that it has rougher terrain than Deimos. Its most spectacular feature is a four-mile-wide crater.

Phobos travels around Mars very quickly, taking only 7 hours and 39 minutes to complete one orbit. Because Mars is spinning on its axis at a slower rate, Phobos travels

A detailed image of Phobos taken by Mariner 9, showing more than a dozen craters.

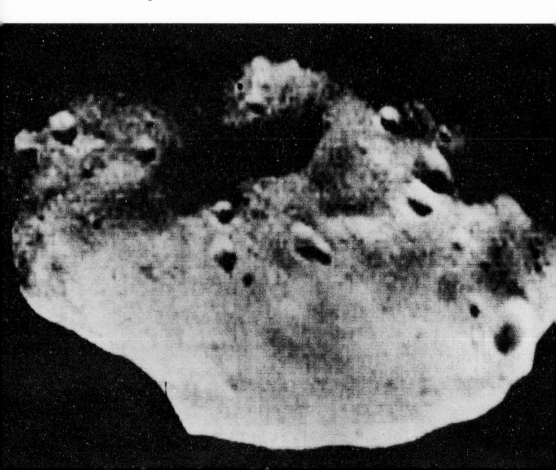

around its parent planet faster than Mars itself rotates. Phobos is unique as the only moon in the solar system to do so. Thus, a person on Mars would see Phobos rise in the east and set in the west three times every Martian day.

The fact that Phobos is apparently approaching Mars accounts for its short period of revolution. Astronomers think that some 4.5 million years ago its orbital period was about 17 hours. The chances are that in another 35 or 40

A view of Deimos taken by Mariner 9, showing
two large craters near the shaded, night side of the moon.

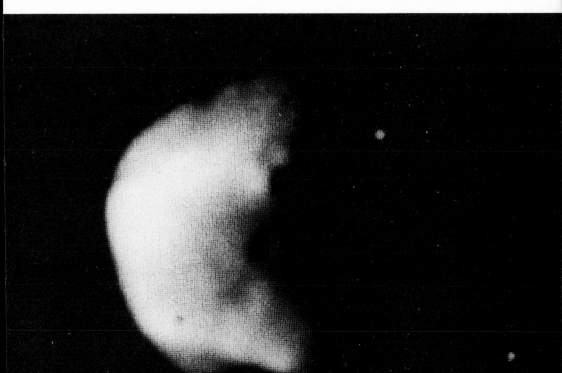

million years Phobos will end its life, either by breaking apart under the gravitational strain of its primary or by crashing into the Martian surface.

The outer satellite, Deimos, is even smaller than Phobos, probably no more than 7 or 8 miles in diameter. The Mariner 9 photographs show that it possesses craters. A person on Mars would not see this miniature world even as a disk. Rather it would look more like a bright star.

Deimos is much farther from Mars than Phobos, about 14,600 miles from the center of the Red Planet, and it takes 30 hours and 18 minutes to orbit Mars once. It revolves around its parent planet more slowly than Mars itself rotates on its axis. Thus, Deimos would seem to rise reluctantly in the east and set slowly in the west. In fact, so slow is Deimos's motion across the Martian sky that before it sets the little moon remains in the sky for more than 60 hours. By comparison, Phobos takes only 4½ hours to cross the Martian sky. Unlike Phobos, Deimos seems to be slowly receding from Mars instead of approaching it.

For most of the Martian year, the two moons would be visible only in the morning or evening twilight, for they would be either invisible against the daytime sky or obscured by the shadow of Mars cast by the sun. Only in midsummer or midwinter would they avoid the shadow long enough to be seen to make an entire trip across the sky. By comparison with our own moon, the masses of these small satellites are small indeed. Their gravitational force must be so feeble that an earthman of average weight would weigh only a few ounces on either satellite.

Astronomers are puzzled about the two little moons. Their tiny size and closeness to Mars are hard to explain. How did they get there, and where did they come from? One explanation is that they are captured asteroids. Perhaps during its early history, Mars was able to capture the two bodies as they came within its gravitational pull.

JUPITER
AND ITS
TWELVE MOONS

Jupiter, the fifth planet from the sun, is the largest in the solar system. In fact, it is much larger than all the other planets combined. Its diameter is a vast 88,700 miles, which is eleven times that of the earth. Its mean distance from the sun is 484,300,000 miles.

Jupiter's orbit lies between the orbits of Mars and Saturn. Its period of revolution is 11.86 years, or nearly 12 of our own earth years. Considering its huge size, Jupiter spins about its axis unusually swiftly. Its rotational period of only 9 hours and 50 minutes makes the Jovian day shorter than any other planet's in the sun's family. The planet's high rotational speed causes the greater amount of matter at its equator to bulge outward, which, in turn, causes a flattening at the poles.

The composition of the giant planet is not solid and rocky like that of the earth and Mars. Scientists know this for two reasons. First, Jupiter has a very low density, only 1.34 that of water. Second, scientists have measured the rotational periods of different regions of the planet and found that they are spinning in slightly varying lengths of time; some are rotating faster than others. This means that Jupiter does not rotate about its axis as a solid body, but as a gaseous, loosely knit one.

If Jupiter is not a solid, rocky planet, what then is it composed of? Scientists disagree as to the internal structure of Jupiter. Some believe it has a rocky core overlaid by ice layers, which, in turn, are overlaid by dense hydrogen. Others maintain that the entire planet consists mainly of hydrogen.

Yet scientists do know more about Jupiter's atmosphere. By analyzing the sun's reflected light from Jupiter—a process called "spectroanalysis"—they believe that the outer Jovian surface is composed of gases, chiefly hydrogen and hydrogen compounds such as methane with some ammonia. Helium also seems to be present. If there is any water, it is solid ice, because the planet is so far from the sun that its surface temperature is very low, perhaps minus 200 degrees Fahrenheit.

It is also obvious to scientists that the Jovian surface is in a disturbed state. The most prominent features on its disk are several light and dark belts, or bands, which are parallel to the equator. These are seen to change constantly in width and shading. Spots are also observed on Jupiter's disk. The best known of these is the Great Red Spot, which seems to be more or less permanent. However, its position is not fixed

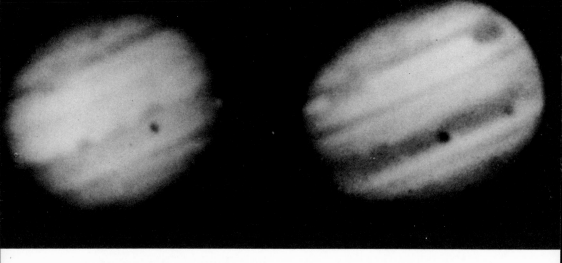

Two photographs of Jupiter.
The one at right shows the Great Red Spot.
A satellite and its shadow can be seen on both.

but drifts about within certain limits. One astronomer believes it is a solid body—perhaps solid helium—floating in the cloudy outer atmosphere of the planet. Another theory suggests there is some large obstruction on the Jovian surface around which the gaseous atmosphere circulates and that the Spot is merely the top of this gaseous column.

As may be imagined, Jupiter's mass is high—nearly 317 times that of earth's. Its surface gravity is 2.64 times that of earth. Thus, a man who weighs 150 pounds on earth would weigh 396 pounds on Jupiter. With such an increase in weight, a man would find it hard to move about on the surface of the planet, if indeed Jupiter has a well-defined "surface" at all below its chilly, swirling gas clouds.

Despite Jupiter's low density, its vast size and great mass give it the powerful gravitional attraction it needs to "hang on" to one small and four large inner moons and seven more quite a distance out from the planet.

With its twelve known satellites, Jupiter possesses more companions in space than any other major planet. The first to be discovered, in 1610, were the four largest and brightest. They are known as the Galilean satellites because the Italian scientist, Galileo Galilei, was the man who glimpsed them first.

On January 7, 1610, Galileo happened to turn his home-made telescope toward Jupiter. He was surprised to observe three bright objects near the planet, two on one side and one on the other. The next night he found that the three objects were in different positions, and all were on the same side of Jupiter. As he watched, one of the three "stars"— for this is what he first thought them to be—disappeared around the edge of the planet. A few nights later he saw four objects where before there had been three.

Soon Galileo deduced that they must be four natural satellites of the planet. They could not be stars, since no stars could make such rapid movements in the heavens because of their great distance from the earth. Galileo's make-

Galileo with his home-made telescope.

shift telescope was not strong enough to pick up the other Jovian moons. Even so, it was powerful enough so that Galileo could make sufficient measurements to calculate the periods of revolution of the four satellites with surprising accuracy.

Galileo's discovery of the four largest moons of Jupiter came at a favorable time in the history of science. According to Aristotle and other ancient sages, all things including the planets and sun revolved around the earth, which was at rest. Men of Galileo's day still held this belief, although some sixty years earlier the great Polish astronomer Copernicus stated that the earth as well as the planets circled the sun. Galileo's discovery was particularly important because it showed that there could be a center of motion (Jupiter and its moons) that is in turn in motion (as Jupiter itself was known to be around the sun). Up to the time of Galileo's discovery of the Jovian moons, it had been argued that if the earth *were* in motion, the moon would be left behind because it could hardly keep up with a rapidly moving planet. Yet here were Jupiter's satellites doing just that!

Soon after Galileo's discovery, the same four satellites were found independently by Simon Marius, a German astronomer. Marius gave them the mythological names of Io, Europa, Ganymede, and Callisto, in order of increasing distance from Jupiter. These names were not officially recognized until much later; by now they have come into accepted usage. Many astonomers, however, prefer the Roman numeral designations of I, II, III, IV, which were given the Galilean satellites in order of their discovery.

The Roman numeral system was also followed as the remaining eight moons were discovered. Due to greater size and visibility some were not discovered in order of their distance from Jupiter. The order of the satellites outward from the planet is: V, I, II, III, IV, VI, VII, X, XII, XI,

VIII, and IX. Although a British astronomer, Brian Marsden, gave the other eight moons additional mythological names, these remain unofficial.

Jupiter's four largest moons can be seen easily with a small telescope or even with a good pair of binoculars. They range in diameter from about 1800 miles to 3200 miles. The two largest, Ganymede and Callisto, are about the size of Mercury (3100 miles) and would be counted as planets in their own right if they did not revolve around Jupiter. Astronomers used to think that Callisto was slightly larger than Ganymede, but more recent measurements show it to be smaller.

The four Galileans move about Jupiter in almost circular orbits that are nearly in the same plane as Jupiter's equator and its own orbit around the sun. Since Jupiter's orbit and that of the earth are also nearly in the same plane, the paths of the Galilean moons appear edgewise to observers on earth. Therefore, the four satellites are seen to swing back and forth from one side of Jupiter to the other, as, in fact, Galileo had observed.

Because the Galileans are so nearly in the plane of Jupiter's equator and their periods of revolution are quite short, Jupiter (as observed from earth) occults, eclipses, or is eclipsed by one or more of the four moons almost daily; only IV, because of its greater distance, can some-

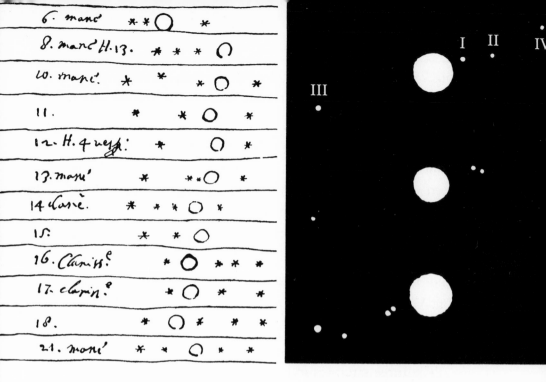

Left: *Galileo's drawings of positions of Jupiter's four large satellites.* Right: *Three exposures showing changes in positions of the four largest and brightest satellites of Jupiter.*

times miss. When one of the satellites goes into the shadow of Jupiter, it becomes invisible. This phenomenon is called an "eclipse." When a satellite is hidden by Jupiter itself instead of by its shadow, the event is called an "occultation."

When one of the Galileans passes between the sun and Jupiter, its shadow can be seen easily in a telescope as a

49

black dot moving across the planet's disk. This movement is known as a shadow transit. The transit of a moon itself is more difficult to observe because the moon looks so much like the surface of Jupiter. Due to their vastly greater distance from the primary, the outer Jovian satellites are seen to occult, eclipse, and transit far less often than the Galileans.

As can be seen in the accompanying diagram, Jupiter's moons fall naturally into three distinct groups. The first and innermost group contains the four Galileans and Satellite V (Amalthea). The latter had escaped discovery until 1892 because of its small size and nearness to the bright planet.

The three satellites in the second group are VI, VII, and X. Orbiting Jupiter at a distance of roughly $7\frac{1}{4}$ million miles, they all have periods of about 250 days. Their orbits are more elliptical than the innermost group and are inclined about 30 degrees to Jupiter's equator.

Moons XII, XI, VIII, and IX form the outermost group. All four are about 14 million miles out from the planet and have periods of approximately two earth years. Their orbits are quite elliptical and are inclined about 150 degrees to Jupiter's equator. The most interesting fact about these outer moons is that their orbital motion is retrograde, or backwards; that is, they do not go from west to east around

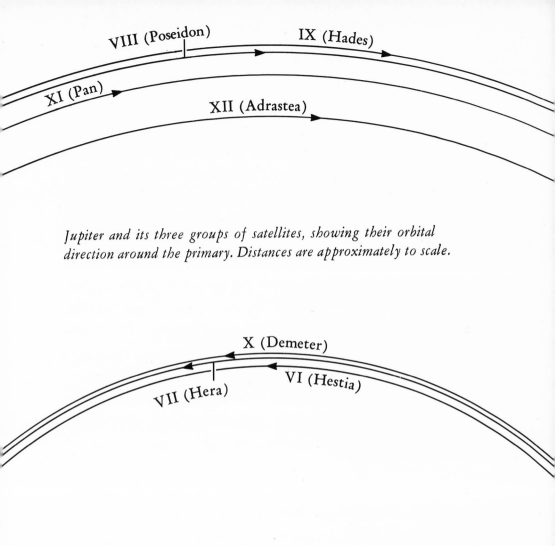

VIII (Poseidon)   IX (Hades)

XI (Pan)

XII (Adrastea)

Jupiter and its three groups of satellites, showing their orbital
direction around the primary. Distances are approximately to scale.

X (Demeter)

VII (Hera)   VI (Hestia)

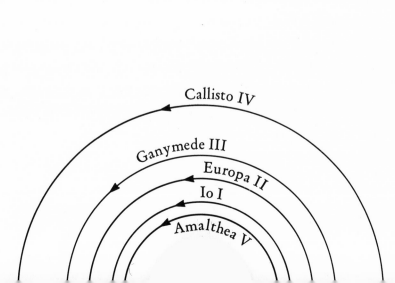

Callisto IV

Ganymede III

Europa II

Io I

Amalthea V

their primary as do their sister moons, but from east to west. Many astronomers believe this course is no coincidence. They think that these moons are not satellites at all, but asteroids captured by Jupiter's powerful gravitational pull from their original orbits between Mars and Jupiter.

Within the two outer groups, the moons' orbits loop through each other. However, the moons in each group move in paths that are so elliptical and angled to each other that they are always a considerable distance apart.

The Jovian satellites are described below in the order of their increasing distance from the parent planet. (Except for the Galilean satellites and Amalthea, the names given are unofficial, following Brian Marsden's system of naming moons after mythological characters.)

Satellite V (Amalthea). This moon was discovered in 1892 by the American astronomer Edward Barnard and is sometimes called Amalthea, the name Barnard gave it. Closer than any of the four Galileans to its primary, V is only about 112,000 miles from Jupiter's center and approximately 68,000 miles from its surface. With a period of revolution of only 12 hours, Amalthea has the greatest orbital velocity of any known satellite. Because of its speed and nearness to Jupiter, it is subject to tremendous gravitational strain, and some astronomers think it may be egg-shaped. However, no photographic proof of its shape exists.

Estimates of V's diameter range from 70 to 150 miles. Its density and composition are unknown.

Satellite I (Io). One of the four Galileans, Io is the third largest, with estimates of its diameter ranging from about 2000 to 2300 miles. It is believed to be a rocky body similar to our moon, with a mass estimated at 1.2 of the moon's (assuming the moon's mass is taken at unity, or 1). Io's density is quite high—4.1 compared to water. The moon takes 1 earth day and $18\frac{1}{2}$ hours to orbit Jupiter. Its mean distance from the planet is about 262,000 miles. G. P. Kuiper thinks that an "excess of metals" may be present in Io, possibly covered with a layer of oxide smoke. Other astronomers believe that because Io reflects light so well it may be covered with a layer of frost.

Satellite II (Europa). Europa is the smallest of the Galileans, with estimates of its diameter ranging from about 1800 miles to 2000 miles. It, also, is thought to be a rocky body like the moon and is denser than the moon at 4.1 compared with water. Its period of revolution is 3 days, 13 hours, and 14 minutes, and its mean distance from Jupiter is about 416,000 miles. Also like Io, it is an excellent reflector of light. Kuiper has suggested that Europa has "at least a partical snow cover," but this has not been corroborated by other scientists.

Satellite III (Ganymede). The largest of the Galileans,

III has an estimated diameter of between 3000 and 3200 miles. At a mean distance of about 664,000 miles from Jupiter, Ganymede takes 7 days, 3 hours, and 43 minutes to revolve around its primary. Much less dense than its Galilean sisters, III's density is 2.4 compared to water.

New evidence reveals that III has a very thin atmosphere. An occultation by Ganymede—its passage in front of a star—occurred in mid-1972. The star's light gradually became extinct. A sharp solid edge of the moon would give an abrupt cutoff, but the gradual decline in light showed that an atmosphere of increasing thickness passed before the star. Some scientists think III may have a rocky core.

Satellite IV (Callisto). Callisto is the second largest—and the outermost—of the Galilean satellites. Estimates of its diameter range from about 2900 miles to 3100 miles. Orbiting Jupiter at a mean distance of about 1,170,000 miles, its period of revolution is 16 earth days, 16 hours, and 32 minutes. Although IV is about the same size as Ganymede, it has the lowest density of all the Galileans—only about 1.9 compared to water. It is unlikely that it retains any atmosphere. Callisto's low reflecting power makes it the faintest of the Galileans. Some scientists think that Callisto is a body of pure ice.

Satellite VI (Hestia). Hestia was discovered in 1904 by the French astronomer Charles Perrine. At a mean distance of about 7,130,000 miles from Jupiter, it revolves around the planet in about 250 earth days. Estimates of its diameter range all the way from 30 to 100 miles. However, VI is by far the largest of the outer Jovian moons. No sound estimates have been made of its density or composition.

Satellite VII (Hera). Hera was discovered by Perrine in 1905. Estimates of its diameter range widely—from as small as 6 miles to as high as 35 miles. At a mean distance of about 7,300,000 miles from its primary, VII orbits Jupiter in about 259 earth days. Its density and physical composition are unknown.

Satellite X (Demeter). The American astronomer S. B. Nicholson discovered Demeter in 1938. Among the smallest of Jupiter's moons, it has a diameter estimated to be from 4 to 15 miles. X revolves about Jupiter at a mean distance of about 7,300,000 miles and takes 259 days to make one revolution. Neither its density nor its composition is known.

Satellite XII (Adrastea). Discovered in 1951 by Nicholson, Adrastea was the last of the Jovian moons to be found. XII revolves in retrograde motion about Jupiter at a mean distance of about 13,000,000 miles and does so once every 631 earth days. It may be the smallest of Jupiter's satellites, with estimates of its diameter ranging from 4 to 14 miles. Its density and composition are unknown.

Satellite XI (Pan). This tiny moon, known as Pan, was

discovered by Nicholson in 1938. It revolves in retrograde motion around Jupiter at a mean distance of about 14,000,-000 miles, making one complete revolution in about 692 days. Estimates of its diameter range between 6 and 19 miles. Pan's density and composition are unknown.

Satellite VIII (Poseidon). Poseidon, was first seen by P. J. Melotte, in England, in 1908. It travels in retrograde motion around its primary at a mean distance of about 14,600,000 miles. Its period of revolution is about 740 days. Estimates of its diameter run from 9 miles to 35 miles. Nothing is known of its density or composition.

Satellite IX (Hades). Hades, the outermost of all the Jovian moons, was discovered by Nicholson in 1914. Orbiting its primary at an immense mean distance of some 14,700,000 miles, IX takes 758 earth days to complete its journey around Jupiter, and it travels in retrograde motion. Estimates of its diameter run from 6 to 17 miles. Nothing is known of its density or composition.

SATURN
AND ITS
TEN MOONS

Beautiful, ringed Saturn is the sixth planet from the sun. Second only to Jupiter in size, its diameter is 75,000 miles, or 9½ times that of the earth. This giant body takes 29½ earth years to complete one revolution around the sun. It rotates on its axis only slightly less rapidly than Jupiter, completing a day in only 10 earth hours and 14 minutes. It revolves about the sun at a mean distance of 886 million miles.

Saturn's mass, though 95 times greater than the earth's, is low for its size. Its density is only .71 that of water. Saturn is the least dense of all the planets despite its great size. Thus, if there were an ocean big enough to hold it, Saturn would float in water! Saturn's low mass causes its surface gravity to be low—only 1.13 that of the earth's. Should an earthman be transferred to the Saturnian surface, he would find his weight only slightly increased.

Like Jupiter, Saturn does not rotate as a solid body but as a gaseous, loosely knit one, and its rapid rotation produces a bulge at the equator and a corresponding flattening at the poles. So distant is the planet from the sun that it receives only 1/90 of the sunlight per unit area as that of the earth. As a result, Saturn has a very low surface temperature of approximately minus 243 degrees Fahrenheit.

What we see of Saturn as it shines brightly in the night sky is the outer part of its atmosphere. It is a gaseous one composed chiefly of hydrogen and hydrogen compounds such as methane and ammonia. Scientists can only speculate about the internal composition of the planet. Some think it may be solid hydrogen. Dark bands, or belts, of gaseous atmospheric currents can be seen across Saturn's disk, but they are less prominent than Jupiter's. Spots are comparatively rare but can be quite striking. Such spots are important to astronomers because by timing their rate of movement across the disk they can find out which portions of the planet are rotating faster or slower than others.

Saturn owes both its beauty and uniqueness in the sun's family to its system of rings. They were first seen by Galileo in the same year that he discovered the four large Jovian moons. The rings have an overall diameter of about 171,000 miles. Their innermost edge is about 7000 miles from the planet's surface. So thin is the ring system that it cannot be accurately measured from as far away as earth. But astronomers have estimated its thickness to be between 10 and 20 miles.

The ring system is chiefly in three concentric parts. The

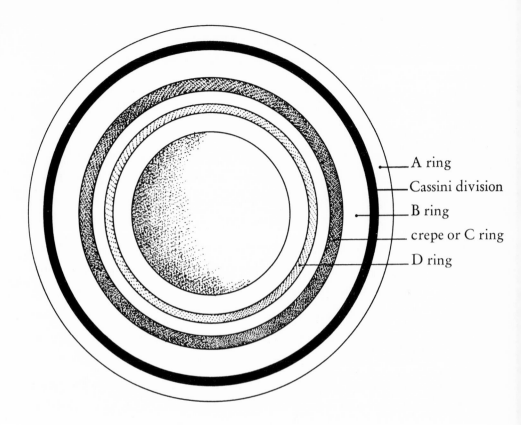

A bird's-eye view of Saturn's ring system. Not drawn to scale.

innermost section is known as the crepe ring, or C ring; the next section is the bright, or B, ring; the outermost is the A ring. Because it is faint, the crepe ring can be seen only in large telescopes and was unknown before 1850. The 2500-mile gap between the A and B rings is called the "Cassini division" in honor of the astronomer C. D. Cassini, who was the first to see and describe it in 1675. Late in 1969, Pierre Guèrin, a French scientist, discovered a fourth, faint ring, D, inside the crepe ring. However, it is not considered official, since some astronomers are doubtful of its existence.

What are Saturn's rings composed of? Scientists think they are swarms of very tiny particles, probably coated with ice, that are variously the size of dust, sand, and gravel— all moving around the planet in the manner of dwarf moonlets. Their size can only be guessed at from how well they reflect light back to earth, with small particles offering a greater total reflecting surface than an equal quantity of large particles. Astronomers know that the rings are not continuous surfaces, or sheets, because their inner parts have been seen to revolve about Saturn in less time than the outer parts.

Saturn's rings lie exactly in the plane of its equator. However, unlike Jupiter, which has very little tilt to its axis, Saturn's axis is tilted a large 28 degrees to the orbit of the earth (used as a basis for comparison). Because of Saturn's tilt, an observer on earth seems to see the rings change from a straight line, when viewed edgewise, to a full circle as Saturn goes through its 29½-year period of revolution. One proof of the thinness of the rings is that they cannot be seen even in powerful telescopes when they are edgewise to earth. The next edgewise view of Saturn's rings will occur in 1980, as shown in the accompanying diagram depicting the changing aspects of Saturn's rings.

Left: *Saturn, photographed at the Lowell Observatory, Flagstaff, Arizona.* Right: *Saturn's changing rings as they appear from earth. Note that the next edge-on view will occur in 1980.*

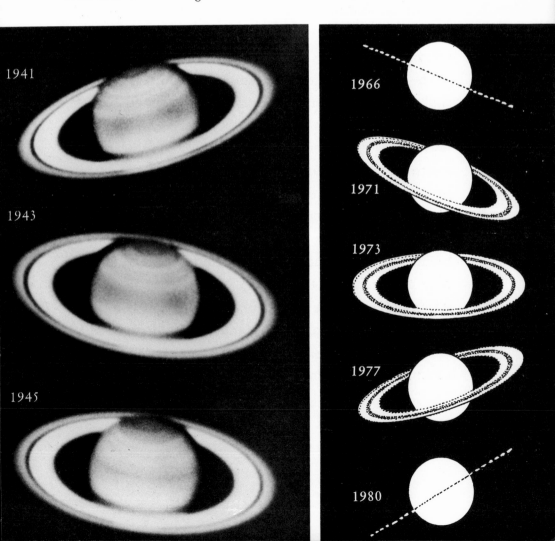

The origin of Saturn's rings has puzzled astronomers for many years. Some think they may be due to a former satellite that came too close to the planet and broke up under the stress of its gravitational attraction. Others think it equally as likely that the ring particles are merely material that never came together to form one body.

Besides the countless tiny satellites that comprise Saturn's rings, ten moons of a more orthodox variety orbit the big planet. Before 1966, it was thought there were only nine, but in that year when there was an edgewise presentation of Saturn's rings, the tenth, Janus, was discovered.

The ten known Saturnian moons were discovered generally in order of their largeness and brightness. Fortunately, the confusing system of Roman numerals was avoided in favor of naming them after mythological characters. The innermost moon is Janus. After Janus, in increasing distance from their primary, come Mimas, Enceladus, Tethys, Dione, Rhea, Titan, Hyperion, Iapetus, and finally Phoebe.

The six innermost satellites form a distinct group, all having nearly circular orbits in the same plane as Saturn's rings. Farther out, the largest (Titan) and the second smallest (Hyperion) are more or less companions, with orbits within less than 200,000 miles of each other. Much farther out is Iapetus, and the most remote is Phoebe, each circling Saturn in lonely orbits millions of miles from their

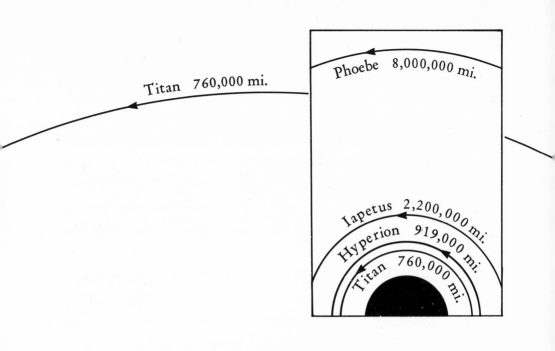

Phoebe   8,000,000 mi.

Iapetus   2,200,000 mi.

Hyperion   919,000 mi.

Titan   760,000 mi.

Titan   760,000 mi.

*Orbits of the Saturnian satellites. Inset shows the great
distance of Phoebe, even from its nearest neighbor, Iapetus.
Distances are approximately to scale.*

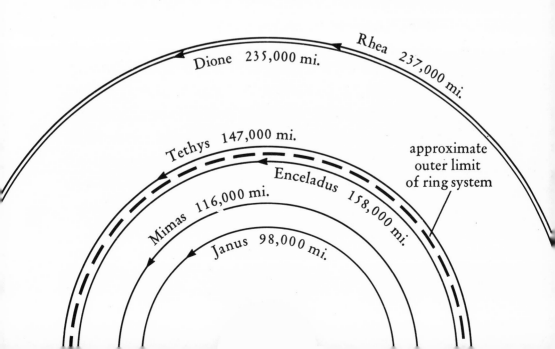

Rhea   237,000 mi.

Dione   235,000 mi.

Tethys   147,000 mi.

Enceladus   158,000 mi.

Mimas   116,000 mi.

Janus   98,000 mi.

approximate
outer limit
of ring system

primary. Some astronomers believe that all of Saturn's moons rotate on their axes so as to present the same face to the planet, as our moon does to the earth.

The Saturnian satellites are described below in the order of their increasing distance from the planet.

Janus. Discovered by the French astronomer Audouin Dollfus in 1966, Janus may be the smallest of Saturn's moons. Estimates of its diameter range from 150 miles to 220 miles. Janus orbits the parent planet at a distance of only 98,000 miles, completing one revolution in about 18 hours. So close is Janus to Saturn that it is highly elusive. It could only be spotted by Dollfus in 1966, the last year in which the rings were presented edgewise to earth, because it is impossible to observe except when the rings are virtually out of view. Janus will not be seen again until 1980, when the rings will again be edgewise to observers on earth. The moon's density and composition are unknown.

Mimas. Discovered by the English astronomer Sir William Herschel in 1789, Mimas, once thought to be the innermost satellite, is now known to be the second moon out from Saturn. Its mean distance from the planet is about 116,000 miles, and it completes one revolution around the primary in 22½ earth days. Estimates of its diameter range between 335 and 400 miles. Mimas may have a density less than that of water, in which case it would float in water.

Little is known of its composition except that some astronomers think it may be icy in nature.

Enceladus. This satellite was also discovered by Herschel at the time he discovered Mimas. At a mean distance of about 158,000 miles from Saturn, it revolves around the parent planet in 1 day and 9 hours. Enceladus's diameter may be anywhere between 275 and 500 miles. Like Mimas, its density may be less that that of water and its composition may be icy.

Tethys. This moon was discovered by Cassini in 1684. It is larger than Janus, Mimas, and Enceladus, with estimates of its diameter running between 600 and 700 miles. But like Mimas and Enceladus, its density may be less than that of water and its composition may be icy in nature. At a mean distance of about 147,000 miles from Saturn, it revolves around the planet in 1 day, 21 hours, and 18 minutes.

Dione. Dione was also found by Cassini in 1684. At a mean distance from Saturn of about 235,000 miles, it completes one revolution around the planet in 2 days, 17 hours, and 41 minutes. Dione's diameter may be anywhere between 300 miles and 600 miles. However, at 3.2 it is probably the densest of all the Saturnian moons, which is about the density of our moon. Dione's composition is unknown.

Rhea. Also discovered by Cassini, in 1672, Rhea is larger

than any of the other moons whose orbits lie closer to Saturn than its own. Its estimated diameter is between 800 and 1000 miles. At a mean distance of about 237,000 miles from Saturn, it completes one revolution of the planet in 4 days, 12 hours, and 25 minutes. Its density compared to water is about 1.9. Nothing definite is known of Rhea's composition.

Titan. Of the ten Saturnian satellites, Titan is the most important. Of planetary size, it is the largest of the group and is the only satellite in the solar system definitely known to have an atmosphere. .Estimates of its diameter range between 2700 and 3500 miles. At either extreme its size is comparable with that of Mercury (3100 miles), and it is a good deal larger than our moon. Titan revolves in an almost circular orbit about Saturn at a mean distance of about 760,000 miles, taking about 16 earth days. Faint surface details have been detected on Titan's disk with very large telescopes. Titan's density is 2.3. The satellite was found by the Dutch astronomer Christian Huygens in 1655.

Brightest of Saturn's moons, Titan was first discovered to have an atmosphere by Kuiper in 1944. Using spectroscopic methods—that is, by analyzing the sunlight reflected from Titan—Kuiper found that the satellite had a thin atmosphere of methane and some ammonia. Until recently, Kuiper and other scientists believed Titan had a forbiddingly low surface temperature, some 180 degrees below zero Fahrenheit. At approximately 900 million miles from the sun, Titan would receive only about 1 percent of the sunlight that the earth gets.

But in 1972, new findings were announced concerning Titan, which were largely the result of the work by Carl Sagan, an American astronomer, of Cornell University. Most startling of the findings was that Titan's atmosphere is apparently not as cold as scientists previously thought it to be—possibly 90 degrees below Fahrenheit at the lowest. Such temperatures are not much colder than those at the earth's North Pole. Because of its temperature and because of certain processes he believes are taking place in the satellite, Sagan thinks that Titan may be hospitable to some form of life in the future. Other scientists besides Sagan are not dismissing the possibility that some elementary life form might eventually emerge there.

"It cannot be the kind of life we know on earth," Dr. Sagan said in a press report, "but it would be earth chauvinism to think that no form of life whatsoever could survive so far off in the solar system. At the very least Titan should be littered with the kinds of organic molecules which, in the early history of the earth, led to the origin of life."

While no one knows for sure how hot the surface of Titan really is, Dr. Sagan believes that it is sufficiently warm for life-producing processes to be under way. He thinks the following is happening on Saturn's seventh moon:

Two important products exist there. One is molecular hydrogen, the most abundant molecule in the universe and present in great quantities in Titan's atmosphere. (Hydrogen molecules consists of two atoms, as in the H_2O of water; they readily combine with other elements and release heat energy.) Molecular hydrogen is responsible for the "greenhouse effect" that causes Titan to be much hotter than it should be at such a great distance from the sun. Basically, the greenhouse effect means that heat is retained on the surface of a planet or satellite by an atmosphere that traps portions of the sun's radiation; without an atmosphere, such a body would quickly lose this radiant energy into space. The greenhouse effect caused by the earth's atmosphere keeps our planet's temperature above the freezing point of water.

The second product, organic compounds that may give rise to primitive life, is known to be produced under laboratory conditions that approximate the conditions believed to exist on Titan. In such laboratory experiments, a reddish-brown chemical compound of complex organic molecules is always produced. This compound is of special interest to Sagan because a dense cloud layer that surrounds Titan's atmosphere exhibits a similar reddishness.

Dr. Sagan believes Titan is made up almost entirely of

chemical ice—methane, ammonia, hydrogen, and water—except for a small molten core of radioactive rock. This core melts the ice far below the surface, forcing liquid layers of methane, ammonia, and water to Titan's surface, much as molten lava rises to the surface of volcanoes on earth. When these liquids burst into a brilliant red on contact with the sun's ultraviolet light, gases are produced. The gases then enter the Titanian atmosphere where they are further broken down by the sun's ultraviolet light into the molecular hydrogen and organic compounds which Dr. Sagan thinks exist on the surface.

Sagan concludes, "Thus the picture that emerges is of a Titan with methane, ammonia, and water being belched forth from volcanoes; organic compounds raining out of the sky; hydrogen produced which, through the greenhouse effect, keeps the surface warm; and large quantities of hydrogen rapidly escaping into space from the top of the Titanian atmosphere. . . . We see Titan as a red disk through the telescopes, which is exactly what we get in the laboratory when we react methane, hydrogen, water ice, and ammonia with ultraviolet rays."

If Dr. Sagan's interesting theory should prove to be true, there exist on this largest Saturnian moon the potential building blocks that gave rise to life on earth.

Hyperion. One of the smaller, fainter Saturnian moons,

Hyperion was discovered by the American astronomer W. C. Bond in 1848. Its diameter is estimated between 200 and 250 miles. Orbiting the primary at a mean distance of about 919,000 miles, it completes one revolution of Saturn in 21 days, 6 hours, and 31 minutes. Despite its small size, Hyperion is fairly dense—3.0 compared to water. But nothing definite is known of its composition.

Iapetus. This moon was discovered by Cassini in 1671. Its diameter is questioned by astronomers. Estimates range from 300 to 1500 miles. At a mean distance of some 2,200,000 miles from Saturn, it moves slowly in its large orbit, completing one revolution in 79 days and nearly 8 hours. Its density and composition are unknown.

Iapetus is one of the most interesting members of Saturn's family, because it varies sharply and strangely in brightness. When it is west of Saturn, it reflects much more sunlight than it does on the planet's eastern side. Some astronomers think that perhaps the moon has a synchronous rotation on its axis; that is, it spins only once in the same time that it takes to go around Saturn once. If so, the brightness variations could be explained by one of its hemispheres reflecting light better than the other. One astronomer suggests that in the remote past Iapetus was either discolored by a gaseous outburst from Saturn or disfigured by a passing celestial body. Other scientists have speculated that it has an atmosphere that freezes when it is behind Saturn and out of the sun. When Iapetus appears on the western side, the sun strikes it on the frozen atmosphere; this highly reflective surface would account for the greater brightness on that side. However, many astronomers do not think Iapetus has an atmosphere, which leads them to believe that the satellite is somehow irregular in shape and thus reflects more light on one of its sides.

Phoebe. The outermost of Saturn's satellites, Phoebe was the first moon in the solar system to be discovered by photographic means instead of by telescope. The American astronomer W. H. Pickering recorded it on photographic plates in 1898. Whether it or Janus is the smallest Saturnian moon is not definitely known. Estimates of Phoebe's diameter range from 125 miles to over 150. This little moon is so far from Saturn—over 8 million miles—and from Iapetus, its nearest sister, that one astronomer has referred to Phoebe as "antisocial." It takes a leisurely $1\frac{1}{2}$ years to complete one revolution of its primary.

Phoebe further asserts its independence of its sister moons by moving in a retrograde motion around Saturn; that is, from east to west, in the opposite direction from the others. Also, Phoebe's orbit is tilted very sharply away from Saturn's equator, unlike those of the other satellites. Its density and physical composition are unknown.

URANUS
AND ITS
FIVE MOONS

Far out in the solar system is the seventh planet from the sun, the giant Uranus, which is the fourth largest of the sun's family. Actually the first major planet to be discovered, it was sighted in 1781 by Sir William Herschel. Until then, Saturn had been the outermost of the known planets. Even the ancients had known of Saturn, Jupiter, Mars, Venus, and Mercury, because they could be seen fairly easily with the naked eye.

Uranus, too, can be seen with the naked eye, but before Herschel's observations it had been recorded some twenty times as a star. On the night of March 13, Herschel was observing the stars in the constellation Gemini with a 7-inch telescope he had just made. Suddenly he saw an object that seemed to be a star—but one that showed a disk. Herschel was puzzled, since all true stars are not disks but mere points of light, even when viewed through a telescope.

Observing the unknown celestial body night after night, Herschel noted that it changed position among the stars. Soon he came to the conclusion that this "moving star" was really a comet, and he so described it in the report he sent to the Royal Society, the renowned British scientific body.

Herschel's "comet" was carefully followed by astronomers all over Europe. They noted that it followed an almost circular orbit far outside Saturn's. In time, they came to realize that the new body was indeed a planet, and Herschel was hailed as its discoverer. He named it Georgium Sidus (Georgian Star) after King George III of England. Until about 1850, English astronomers called the planet the Georgian; to others, it was known as Herschel.

Sir William Herschel and his sister, Caroline, who aided the great astronomer in his work, and their telescope.

Its ultimate name—Uranus—was chosen by the German astronomer Johann Bode.

Since there are 5000 stars in the night sky that appear as bright or brighter, it is not surprising that Uranus escaped notice for so long. The cause of its faintness is its great distance from the sun—a mean distance of about 1,783,000,000 miles; this is over 19 times farther from the sun than is the earth. Uranus takes 84 earth years to complete one revolution around the sun, and the planet rotates on its axis once every 10 hours and 45 minutes.

Uranus has a diameter of about 29,300 miles. Its density figure is a little greater than Saturn's—about 1.56 that of water. Despite its size, the planet's surface gravity is only some 7 percent greater than that of earth's. The sunlight on the planet is so weak that its surface temperature is extremely cold, about minus 300 degrees Fahrenheit.

A comparison of the axial tilt of Uranus to that of five other planets.

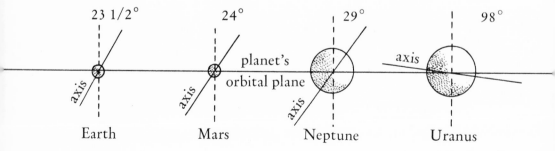

23 1/2°   24°   29°   98°

planet's orbital plane

axis

Earth   Mars   Neptune   Uranus

Uranus is greenish in color and only occasionally shows faint markings like the belts on Jupiter and Saturn. Also like those planets, it has a thick gaseous atmosphere composed of methane and traces of ammonia; hydrogen and helium are also present. Underneath the gaseous atmosphere, astronomers believe there are layers of chemical ice and that the center is a rocky core.

There are two odd facts about Uranus. First, it is the only planet in the solar system to rotate on its axis from east to west; all the others go from west to east. Second, Uranus is tilted at a huge angle to its orbit around the sun, greater than that of any other planet to its orbit. Earth is tilted $23\frac{1}{2}$ degrees, Mars 24, Jupiter only 3, Saturn $26\frac{1}{2}$, Neptune 29. But Uranus is tilted at more than a right angle—98 degrees! Uranus, therefore, goes around the sun lying on its side, instead of orbiting the sun more or less

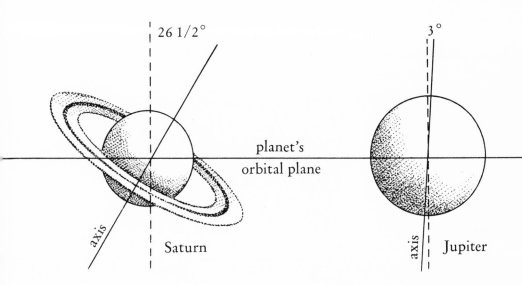

26 1/2°

planet's
orbital plane

axis

Saturn

3°

axis

Jupiter

vertically as the other planets do. In this strange position, the Uranian poles, rather than the equator, alternately face the sun as the planet revolves in its orbit.

This unusual tilt of its axis makes the planet's five moons all the more interesting, because they revolve very nearly in Uranus's equatorial plane. Thus the whole Uranian system is one of a planet "on its side" rushing through space with its moons whirling vertically about it. When either of Uranus's poles is presented to the earth in a bird's-eye view —as it was in 1945 and will be in 1985—the orbits of the moons will appear circular. But in those years when the Uranian equator is presented to earth—as was the case in 1966 and will be in 2007—the orbits of the moons will be seen edgewise; that is, the satellites will be seen to pass back and forth in a straight line from one side of Uranus to the other. In addition, all of the Uranian satellites orbit their primary very rapidly in the same retrograde motion as Uranus rotates; that is, from east to west. Though all five satellites are much smaller than our moon, they are denser and none is thought to have an atmosphere. Unlike other moons of the solar system that were given mythological names, those of Uranus were given poetical ones from literary works.

The Uranian satellites are described below in order of their increasing distance from their primary.

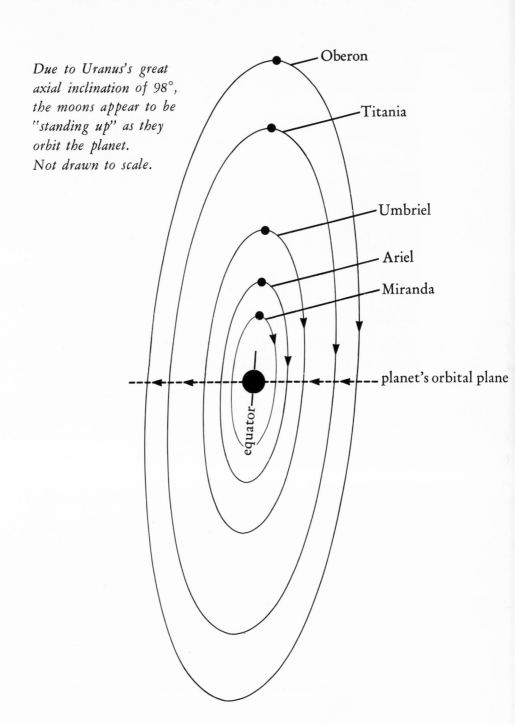

Due to Uranus's great
axial inclination of 98°,
the moons appear to be
"standing up" as they
orbit the planet.
Not drawn to scale.

Oberon

Titania

Umbriel

Ariel

Miranda

planet's orbital plane

equator

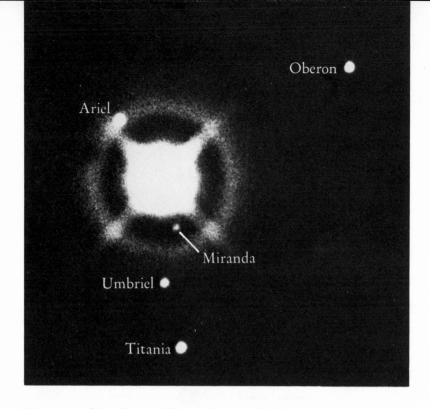

*Uranus and its five satellites photographed at
the McDonald Observatory, Mount Locke, Texas.*

Miranda. The faintest and smallest of the Uranian moons,
Miranda was the fifth and last to be found. Kuiper discovered it in 1948. Miranda orbits Uranus at a mean distance of about 80,000 miles, completing one revolution in
1 day, 9 hours, and about 50 minutes. Estimates of its diameter vary from about 100 to 200 miles. Its density is 5 times
that of water. Nothing definite is known of its physical com-

position. The moon was named after a character in Shakespeare's *The Tempest*.

Ariel. The English amateur astronomer William Lassell found Ariel in 1851. Estimates of its diameter vary greatly, from 400 to 1500 miles. The satellite revolves around Uranus at a mean distance of about 119,000 miles, completing one full revolution in 2 earth days, 2 hours, and 29 minutes. Its density is thought to be about 5 times that of water. Ariel's physical composition is unknown. Lassell named Ariel after a sylph (an imaginary being inhabiting the air) in Alexander Pope's *The Rape of the Lock*.

Umbriel. Lassell also discovered this moon at the same time that he found Ariel. Estimates of its diameter run between 300 and 800 miles. Umbriel's period of revolution takes 4 days, 3 hours, and 28 minutes. It orbits Uranus at a mean distance of about 166,000 miles. Its density is about 4 times that of water. The satellite's composition is unknown. Like Ariel, Umbriel was named for a sylph in Pope's *The Rape of the Lock*.

Titania. Possibly the largest of the Uranian moons, Titania was discovered by Herschel in 1787. Estimates of its diameter run as low as 600 miles to as high as 1500 miles. Titania orbits its primary at a mean distance of about 272,000 miles and completes one revolution in 8 earth days, 16 hours, and 56 minutes. The moon is thought to have the highest density of any in its group, at 6 times that of water. Nothing is known of its composition. Titania was named after the fairy queen in Shakespeare's *A Midsummer Night's Dream.*

Oberon. The outermost of the Uranian satellites, Oberon was discovered by Herschel in the same year he discovered Titania. Its size may be slightly smaller than Titania, with estimates ranging from 700 to 1500 miles. The satellite orbits Uranus at a mean distance of about 364,000 miles. It completes one revolution of the primary in 13 days, 11 hours, and 7 minutes. Its density is thought to be about 5 times that of water. Nothing is known definitely of its physical composition. Oberon was named after the fairy king in Shakespeare's *A Midsummer Night's Dream.*

NEPTUNE
AND ITS
TWO MOONS

Far out in the depths of interplanetary space, a thousand million miles beyond the orbit of Uranus, is the last of the giant planets and the eighth from the sun. It is Neptune. If Uranus seems remote and lonely, Nepune is far more so. If an earthman could stand on the Neptunian surface, he would be able to see little of the solar system apart from the shrunken sun. Saturn and Jupiter would be hard to detect. Earth, Mars, Venus, and Mercury would be invisible. Only Uranus and Pluto would be readily seen when sufficiently close in their orbits to Neptune's.

The story of Neptune's discovery is an interesting one. The planet was literally found on paper—by mathematics. After Herschel found Uranus in 1781, other astronomers watching the planet noticed that it wandered slightly in its orbit. Also, up to the year 1822, Uranus seemed to move too rapidly; after that year, it seemed to lag in its orbit. This phenomenon puzzled astronomers, and it soon became clear that some unknown factor was causing Uranus's strange behavior.

Astronomers had already taken into account the gravitational effects of Jupiter and Saturn on Uranus. But still Uranus wandered. In time, scientists began to think that Uranus's straying from its orbit might be due to the pull of an unknown planet still farther from the sun. Eventually the existence of this new planet was predicted independently by a Frenchman, Urbain J. J. Leverrier, and an Englishman, John C. Adams. Both mathematicians came to nearly identical conclusions in their search for the hypothetical planet.

Adams completed his work first, and it was sent to the British astronomer royal, Sir George Airy. Unfortunately for Adams, Airy gave it little attention. Meanwhile, Leverrier finished his calculations and sent them to Johann Enke in Germany in 1846. On Enke's instructions, the German astronomers Johann G. Galle and Heinrich d'Arrest, at the Berlin Observatory, began searching in the position in the sky given by Leverrier. Almost at once they identified the body now called Neptune. Because Adams's calculations were finished first but Leverrier's led to the discovery, astronomers give credit to both men.

Physically, Neptune is much like Uranus and is sometimes called "Uranus's twin." Before 1966, it was thought that Neptune was the smaller of the two, at a diameter of 27,700 miles. In that year, however, new calculations placed its diameter at 31,500 miles, establishing Neptune as the larger of the two giant planets. Its density is 1.8 times that of water, almost the same as that of Uranus. Neptune's surface gravity, at 1.2 that of earth's, is also almost the same as that of Uranus.

Both Neptune and Uranus show up as greenish disks in the telescope. The surface temperature of Neptune is lower than Uranus's—about minus 360 degrees—because it is farther from the sun. But the composition of the two planets is thought to be similar—largely hydrogen and hydrogen compounds, with methane the important constituent of its gaseous atmosphere. Neptune, too, is believed to have a rocky core surrounded by layers of chemical ice.

Only in its vastly greater distance from the sun does Neptune cease to be "Uranus's twin." Neptune orbits the sun at a mean distance of about 2793 million miles, which is 30 times the distance of earth from the sun. The giant planet takes almost 165 earth years to complete one revolution around the sun. Since its discovery in 1846, it has gone through only about two thirds of a revolution and will not have made a complete one until the year 2011. Yet Neptune is a fast spinner, taking only about 14 hours to rotate on its axis.

The planet has two known satellites. The closest to Neptune, and by far the largest and brightest, is Triton. It was discovered by Lassell very shortly after Neptune itself was found. Estimates of Triton's diameter range between 2300 and 3000 miles, making it larger than our moon.

Triton orbits Neptune at a mean distance of about 220,000 miles, which is about the same distance as our moon from the earth. Triton's period of revolution is very short; it fairly streaks around its giant primary in a brief 5 days and 21 hours. Its density is believed to be about 5 times that of water. The satellite's mass is also high—1.8 times that of our moon. The satellite orbits Neptune in a retrograde direction and is the only large moon in the solar system to have east to west motion. While Triton's orbit is almost circular, it is sharply inclined to Neptune's equator—about 160 degrees.

Because Triton is large and has high density and mass, astronomers think it may have enough gravitational attraction to hold a thin atmosphere. In 1944, Kuiper announced he had found traces of a methane atmosphere by analyzing the reflected sunlight coming from Triton. However, this finding has not been confirmed by other scientists.

One astronomer's calculations indicate that Triton is slowly approaching Neptune and that eventually, in the remote future, the satellite may either collide with its primary or else break up under increasingly severe gravitational strains. Other astronomers have serious doubts about these calculations.

Neptune and its two satellites. Nereid (upper right arrow),
too faint to be observed visually through a telescope, was found
in 1949 after its image was left on photographic plates.

Neptune's second and outermost satellite is Nereid. Too
faint to be observed visually through any existing telescope,
it was found by Kuiper in 1949 only after it had left its
image on photographic plates. Nereid's diameter is uncer-

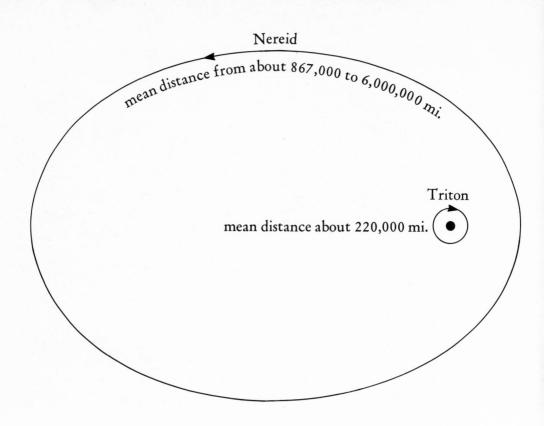

Nereid

mean distance from about 867,000 to 6,000,000 mi.

Triton

mean distance about 220,000 mi.

Orbits of Neptune's two satellites and mean distances from their planet. Note the highly elliptical shape of Nereid's orbit. Distances are approximately to scale.

tain, but most estimates place it at about 200 miles. Nothing is known of the little moon's physical makeup.

The remarkable thing about Nereid is its orbit. It is so elliptical, or "squashed," that during its period of almost

1 earth year, it swings in to Neptune as close as 867,000 miles and then wanders out as far as 6 million miles or more. Its movement around Neptune is from west to east. Some astronomers think that Nereid may be a captured asteroid.

These, then, are the thirty-two known moons of the sun's family. Are they merely dead and useless worlds of frosty rock, locked in lonely orbits around their primaries? Or are they gaseous, potentially developing worlds of the remote future? Of what possible use are these distant satellites that circle planets, which (except for Mars) probably can never be landed on by men?

At this point in time, the moons of the outer giants—Jupiter, Saturn, Uranus, and Neptune—are hopelessly out of range for manned spacecraft from earth. Only unmanned automatic space probes such as those of the Pioneer series, with their cameras electronically poised to send back pictures of "grand tour" expeditions through the solar system, can obtain firsthand information of the outer planets and their moons. As for the Martian moons, they probably need not be landed on at all, for the Red Planet itself is as solid as our own moon and thus can be touched down upon by either manned or robot spacecraft. Very possibly such a landing will be accomplished before the year 2000.

Looking farther ahead, perhaps in a century's time, we can picture the day when manned flights to Jupiter, Saturn, Uranus, and Neptune become possible. Men will land on the satellites of these immense planets and set up lasers, seismometers, cameras, and other equipment in order to study the four largest members of the sun's family. To these astronauts, especially those working on innermost satellites, the planets themselves will appear gigantic and so compellingly dominant in the heavens that men will find it difficult to turn their eyes away from the breathtaking sight.

Perhaps earthmen will choose Ganymede or Callisto from which to study Jupiter; if so, Jupiter will appear to blot out half the sky for much of the time. In the vicinity of Saturn, they may choose Titan or Rhea or Dione. From those moons, astronauts will see the spectacular sight of the rings nearly edgewise, with the innermost satellites rapidly transiting the huge belted disk of Saturn.

Perhaps, to study Uranus, Mission Control will select Titania or Oberon as temporary space stations. Or, in the case of Neptune, astronauts may one day find themselves setting up equipment on that planet's major satellite, Triton. When they pause from their work, they will marvel at their remoteness in the solar system. The sun will be but a brilliant speck in the ebony blackness of interplanetary space. The other major planets, if they can be seen at all, will be hard to detect. Of their home planet earth, nothing will be seen. And inevitably their eyes will be drawn back to the spectacle of the parent planet brooding in the sky and the bitterly cold gas clouds swirling in its atmosphere.

The existence of the thirty-two moons may offer man an unparalled opportunity to win greater knowledge of the solar system in which he lives.

GLOSSARY

asteroid: one of tens of thousands of small planets ranging in size from a few hundred miles to less than a mile in diameter.

atmosphere: the gaseous envelope of a celestial body.

axis: the straight line, real or imaginary, passing through a rotating body and which is the line about which that body rotates.

celestial body: a general term for all objects that can be observed in the sky beyond the earth's atmosphere; the sun, the moon, the planets and their satellites, comets, stars, etc.

cosmic dust: large clouds of fine particles of matter in interstellar space.

density: the amount of matter in a unit volume of a substance.

disk: the seemingly flat figure of a celestial body as it appears in the sky.

ecliptic: the plane of the earth's orbit around the sun.

ellipse: a plane curve on which the sum of the distances from any point of its circumference to two points within, called the foci, is always the same.

gravitation: the force of attraction that exists among all particles of matter everywhere in the universe.

maria (on the moon): large, dark plains on the surface of the moon; misnamed *maria* ("seas" in Latin) by Galileo, because they so appeared to him through his telescope.

mascons: large concentrations of massive material in the moon's crust; an acronym coined by scientists from *mass concentrations.*

mass: a measure of the total amount of matter that a (celestial) body contains.

meteoroid: particles of solid matter that exist in, and move through space; meteoroids can be of any size and composition.

moon: in general, a satellite; specifically, the satellite of the earth; *see* natural satellite.

moonquake: a disturbance in the moon's structure resembling an earthquake on the earth.

natural satellite: a celestial body that revolves around one of the planets of the solar system; *see* moon.

nebula: a vast aggregation of matter at stellar distances that shows as a hazy spot or cloud; a gas cloud in space.

occultation: the hiding of one celestial body by another, as when one of the moons of Jupiter passes behind the planet.

orbit: the path of a body that is in revolution about another body, as a natural satellite about its parent body.

period of revolution: in the solar system, the time required for a celestial body, such as a planet, to make one revolution about the sun; also, the time required for a natural satellite to make one revolution around its primary body.

primary: a planet with respect to its natural satellites; the parent body about which its natural satellites revolve.

protoplanet: in theories of the origin of the solar system, a primordial gaseous mass that condenses, cools, and evolves into the present planets; a planet-to-be.

protosun: in theories of the origin of the solar system, a primordial gaseous mass that evolved into the sun; a sun-to-be.

radioactivity: the spontaneous change in the atoms of certain heavy elements, such as radium and uranium, by which they give off radiation and slowly change into different elements.

refracting minerals: minerals, such as thorium, that melt only at
very high temperatures.

retrograde motion: a natural satellite that moves from east to west
about its primary, instead of from west to east as is normal for
most natural satellites in the solar system.

rotational period: the time required for a planet or similar body
to turn once on its axis; its "day."

shadow transit: the passage of the shadow of a natural satellite
across the disk of its primary.

solar system: the system of the sun and its planets, their satellites,
and other objects revolving around the sun.

sun: the star around which the earth and other planets and their
natural satellites revolve.

INDEX

indicates illustration

Born in Glens Falls, New York, David C. Knight received his education both in this country and abroad. After earning his BA degree at Union College, Schenectady, New York, he spent a year at the Sorbonne, in Paris, then continued his studies at the Engineering Institute, in Philadelphia, and at the University of Pennsylvania.

After serving in the U.S. Army during World War II, Mr. Knight worked as an editor and production man with Prentice-Hall. Later he became senior science editor at Franklin Watts. Science has been one of Mr. Knight's major interests, and he has written twenty-six books on various scientific subjects. He also has written a number of science articles for the *New Book of Knowledge*.

At present Mr. Knight lives in Dobbs Ferry, N.Y., with his wife and two daughters.